KidLit-O Presents's

Princess Diana for Kids

A Biography of Princess Diana Just for Kids!

Sara Presley

KidLit-O Press

www.KidLito.com

Table of Contents

About

KidLit-o was started for one simple reason: our kids. They wanted to find a way to introduce classic literature to their children.

Books in this series take all the classics that they love and make them age appropriate for a younger audience—while still keeping the integrity and style of the original.

We hope you and you children enjoy them. We love feedback, so if you have a question or comment, stop by our website!

Introduction

Perhaps you have heard of the late Princess Diana. Since the moment she was born, she was a member of the British Royal Family, which dates back hundreds of years. Britain, one of the most influential countries in Europe and the world, is ruled by a monarchy. One person, currently Queen Elizabeth of England, is at the head of the entire nation. The royal family are people related to her, and because of this relation, they hold power.

Diana's family always had some ties to royalty in fame throughout Britain, but she joined the royal family through marriage. This tied her to fame and fortune, and a life of lavish luxury. Princess Diana became a role model for girls and women across the world, both for her beauty and her work in charity. To this day, people still discuss the effect that Princess Diana had on the world. In order to understand Diana's legacy, it is important to understand her life, and also what led up to her untimely and shocking death.

Chapter 1: Early Life

Born on the first day of July in 1961, Diana Spencer lived a short, but impactful, life. Two months after she was born, she was christened at the St. Mary Magdalene Church, a popular church for her family. Newborn Diana was born into a family with three other siblings: two older sisters, Jane and Sarah; and one younger brother, Charles.

Diana Spencer and her family lived in a luxurious home called Althorp. While the name might not sound appealing, the home has a rich history. It was constructed in the year 1508 by the Spencer family. The descendants of the owners have held the house ever since, holding nineteen generations of the family. Althorp is open to visitors and tours during the summer, for tourists that may want to see the hundreds of years of history, or see the rooms where Diana played as a child.

Althorp is nestled in Northamptonshire, a part of England that sits on the middle of the island. Diana Spencer was the child of an unhappily married couple. Her father, Johnnie, was the eighth Earl Spencer. *Earl Spencer* is a title that was created in the 1700s for the head of Althorp. Diana's mother, Frances Roche, married Johnnie Spencer and joined the rich Spencer family.

Johnnie Spencer and Frances Roche were married for fourteen years until Frances became interested in another man. Frances wanted a divorce, and the two parents began a custody battle over their four children. Diana, who was only six years old at the time, got caught in the middle.

When the courts tried to decide which parent should get custody of the children, it was a simple decision. While Johnnie was an attentive father, Frances was often too busy with her fame and social status. Because of this, she rarely paid attention to Diana and her siblings.

For a six year old Diana, this ordeal between her mother and father was extremely confusing. Any six-year old would be sad when his or her mother leaves, and so was Diana. She did not know why her mother was leaving. However, she did get the opportunity to stay with her mother on the weekends, so Frances was not totally absent from Diana's life. The divorce, however, was the first of many heartbreaks and emotional crises in Diana's life.

Part of this emotional trouble could have been the cameras that Diana grew up with. A group that always had their cameras trained on her was the *paparazzi*, which are reporters and photographers that try to expose the lives of celebrities. Wherever Diana turned, there was a camera, especially because her father Johnnie loved to take home videos. Diana learned that she needed to smile often and that, if she wanted to stay happy, she needed to love the camera.

But when the young Diana Spencer was not smiling in front of a camera or pulling pranks on her family, she was reading the books of Barbara Cartland. Cartland writes romantic fiction, which Diana was obsessed with. She liked the tales of love, the handsome princes, the beautiful princesses that would be swept off their feet. Diana would read dozens of these books.

For much of her life, Diana had no female role models. While most children might have a supportive mother or grandmother, Diana was not surrounded by good examples. On her father's side, her grandmother Lady Cynthia was remarkably quiet. Not an outspoken woman, she did not have a strong influence on Diana's life and her behavior.

On her mother's side, her grandmother Ruth was incredibly rude and mean to young Diana. Her stepmother Raine did not take a liking towards Diana. And in addition to that, Diana's sisters Jane and Sarah were poorly behaved.

Perhaps because of this, Diana took a turn towards a childhood of poor behavior, especially for a young lady who constantly stood in the public spotlight. Diana was a trickster, and she loved to pull pranks throughout the day. Whether it was torturing her sisters or the nannies that were constantly hired to take care of her, Diana's sense of humor could have been tamed so that the people around her did not get annoyed.

As if that weren't enough, Diana was a spoiled child, following the stereotype of a child born into a rich family. When she did not get what she wanted, she had a tendency to cry or give her father the puppy dog eyes. Most people found it hard to resist such a young, lovely child, especially one who was born into a position of power.

The pranks and tricks only increased when Diana's father, Johnnie Spencer, became flirtatious with another woman. After Frances Roche left, Johnnie wanted another wife, and he was interested in Raine McCorquodale. Once Johnnie and Raine became more serious, Diana was jealous. She was used to always having her father to herself; she didn't want a woman to steal her father away.

Johnnie and Raine married on the 14th of July, 1976. This was just two weeks after Diana Spencer turned fifteen years old. The couple was not interested in a big, grand wedding—as was tradition. Any weddings among the rich were usually not quiet. But the wedding between Johnnie and Raine was so low-key that even Johnnie's children were not invited. This hurt Diana, even if she wouldn't have wanted to see them get married anyway. The wedding hosted one thousand people, but the four Spencer children were not among them.

This sparked harsh rebellion from Diana. She constantly searched for ways to argue with her father. She wrote cruel and mean letters to Raine. She picked up the phone and did prank phone calls. And when Johnnie took away Diana's stereo system, Diana decided to sabotage and damage the family's stereo. If she couldn't listen to hers, no one could.

This does not sound the childhood of a princess. While Diana was not a princess yet, and she never knew she would be, she always imagined it, especially as she read the works of Barbara Cartland, her favorite romantic fiction writer. A funny coincidence is that Raine, who Diana hated more than anything, was Barbara Cartland's daughter.

Perhaps Diana loved the stories of Cartland because they were perfect; in those stories, she did not have to cope with the divorce of her parents and disappearance of her mother. She did not have to see her father torn away from her when he was married to another woman. Diana's emotional troubles started young, and they would continue throughout her life.

Chapter 2: Education

All of Diana's family knew what they wanted to do when they got older—but not Diana. Diana had trouble deciding exactly which direction she wanted her life to go in.

Until she was nine years old, Diana was schooled at Althorp. At the age of nine, Diana was sent to a boarding school called Riddlesworth Hall. This wasn't your normal school, or even your normal boarding school. Riddlesworth Hall took away the stress on academics, and wanted its students to focus more on the social aspects of life. Instead of becoming advanced in math and science, the students were expected to learn conversational skills and express themselves artistically. While this type of school might not have been ideal for any average student in Britain, it was perfect for someone of a high social class. Riddlesworh Hall rests in Norfolk, and only takes students ages nine to twelve.

After she graduated from Riddlesworth Hall, Diana moved onto West Heath, a school in Kent. Both of her sisters had attended West Heath, so it was becoming a tradition among the female children. Like Riddlesworth Hall, West Heath was a place reserved only for female students from twelve to sixteen years of age. West Heath did not see academics as extremely important. For members of royalty and the upper class, for people with lots of money who would spend most of their life before the cameras, social skills were much more important than simple school subjects.

Specifically, Diana had a few talents and interests during her time at Riddlesworth Hall and West Heath. She enjoyed dancing in her ballet classes, and swimming was a favorite sport of hers. Diana tended to be popular among her classmates, because of her good looks, her talkativeness, and her talent in ballet and swimming.

At the age of sixteen, Diana left school. She committed to the duties of a nanny, which had been a tradition in the Earl Spencer's family. Both her mother and her sisters had left school to become nannies. This tradition was not something that Diana minded. Besides, as she admitted, she was not as smart as her sisters. She often joked about this—that she was not as intellectually advanced, and that her sister was.

Diana was not expected her to pursue higher education after she turned sixteen. Her class and social status maintained that she was a woman of family and royalty. This is why her life turned inwards, towards a few years of acting as a nanny. This would prepare her for a family life, which would better suit her.

Chapter 3: Courting, Engagement, and the Wedding

Diana, who was now growing into a young lady, probably kept up with all of the news about Britain's royal family. The Queen of England, Queen Elizabeth II, has been ruling since 1952, when she was only twenty-five years old. Queen Elizabeth II still rules the nation today.

At the time, the Queen's son was looking for a bride. Prince Charles was seeking someone who had not yet been married—someone who wished to devote herself to the royal family.

Prince Charles had dated several people over the course of his younger years, but none of them seemed to be the right match. He dated everyone from celebrities to movie actresses to glamorous magazine models to friends of the family. Interested girlfriends knew that plenty of glamor and fame would come with dating the prince.

As a child, Charles had been upset with the affection he received from his parents. His parents, Queen Elizabeth II and King Philip, loved him, of course; but Charles did not like how little affection his parents were allowed to show in front of the cameras. This could be the reason for Charles's extensive hatred of the paparazzi. The young Charles, however, found affection in his grandmother, the Queen's mother.

Charles also enjoyed spending time with his Uncle Dickie, who served as a substitute for his emotionless father. Uncle Dickie was everything Charles was looking for in a role model: charming, daring, and adventurous. Dickie had spent time taking charge in World War II, something that Charles admired. Queen Elizabeth and King Philip, however, did not like their son spending time with Dickie, because they knew he was a substitute for their own parenting.

As Prince Charles continued dating and exploring the world, he almost dated Tricia Nixon, the daughter of American president Richard Nixon. But Charles's hatred of the paparazzi endured tirelessly as they covered each moment of his relationships. There seemed to be a cycle between Charles and the paparazzi: every time Charles would date someone new, the paparazzi would extensively cover the life of the new girlfriend and search for mistakes or secrets in her past. The newspapers and magazines would rip her apart, painting her in a poor light. The relationship would then fall apart, and Charles was on the search again.

At this point, as Charles burned through several relationships, even Queen Elizabeth became frustrated. She wanted Charles to marry quickly, but she also wanted it to be *just* the right girl. Being the Queen of England, Elizabeth had many grudges and enemies, so she was exceedingly careful to sabotage any relationship that she didn't like. Charles found the pressure to be harrowing, as it was both a race against time and a quest to please his family.

One girl did stand out above the rest, however. In the summer of 1971, Prince Charles met the beautiful Camilla Shand. The two of them hit it off right away. Their courtship lasted a while, until Charles left for an eight-month boating trip. During the trip, Camilla found another man she was interested in, and married him. Of course, Charles was devastated, but the magazines and newspapers of England reported that there may have been old love kindling between Charles and Camilla months later.

And that was when Diana Spencer came into the picture. After years of dating and an on-and-off relationship with Camilla, Diana was a breath of fresh air for Charles. She was cute, young, and charming. Even the selective Queen Elizabeth II took a liking to her, preferring her to almost all other possible girlfriends. Diana was honest, sincere, and quiet—obviously, the Queen had never seen Diana in her home life.

Diana Spencer and Prince Charles met at the prince's thirtieth birthday, when Diana was only seventeen years old. Yet despite the age difference, both Charles and the Queen enjoyed Diana's company and thought she would make a great companion to Charles. Diana stuck in their minds for weeks after the birthday party.

Gradually, Diana began receiving invitations to more royal affairs, such as theater parties and balls. Charles's interest for Diana only grew, and Diana accepted his interest with warm welcome. After all, she had been dreaming of princes and princesses all her life—and here she was, confronted with a prince who might love her one day. It was like a dream come true for Diana!

Members of the royal family, and others who were at the royal affairs, noted how much trouble Diana went to in order to impress Prince Charles. It seemed like she was the perfect match for the searching prince.

Newspapers and magazines exploded when they found out Charles and Diana started dating. It was not just the royal family that loved Diana, but the paparazzi did, as well. Diana was not the typical girlfriend of Charles; she was something special.

People thought Diana was cute and charming, and an image quickly caught on: "Shy Di," the quiet girlfriend who was a friend of everyone. While, in fact, Diana was not shy or quiet, she appeared this way because she lowered her head whenever the paparazzi came around. Whether Diana just pretended to be shy or whether she was dealing with newly-gained fame is unclear. What *is* certain is that Diana knew exactly how to entertain the paparazzi. People *loved* her.

As a member of the royal family, the cameras of magazines and newspapers were constantly surrounding Prince Charles—and now they surrounded Diana, who was now nicknamed "Lady Di." Diana enjoyed the fame: the flashes of cameras bounced off her white teeth, her smile never broke, and her eyes lit up when she was confronted with crowds of reporters, writers, and admirers.

Prince Charles, on the other hand, was not such a fan of the paparazzi, who had been harassing him since he was a child. Little did either of them know that the paparazzi would become such a powerful part of Diana's life that they would eventually lead to her death.

After Diana and Charles began dating, the media began judging their relationship. Diana and Charles never shared public affection, and this was in part because Charles had never been shown affection, or even shown affection in public by his parents. While many people speculated that Diana and Charles did not seem close because of all the cameras trained on them, others rumored that Diana and Charles were not *actually* in love.

Like most men in the royal family and who work in government, Charles was constantly torn between work and his private life. Diana rarely ever saw her new boyfriend, especially since he went on extensive trips around the world. His trips were partly business, and partly escapes from the tough life of the British government.

Normally, Diana would not have been so upset about his trips; but the thing was that Charles never called her. When he would come home from his tours across the globe, the couple would only see each other in public. It was exceedingly rare for them to ever meet in private, something that caused damage to their relationship.

However, despite all of the communication issues that Charles and Diane faced, she still wanted to marry him. For weeks, Diana anxiously waited for Charles to propose to her. After all, she was supposed to be living the life of a princess now, and she wanted to marry her boyfriend. Perhaps Diana was not truly in love with him, but loved the glamor and fame and royalty that would come with marrying Charles.

Finally, after much pressure from the Queen and the rest of his family, Prince Charles finally popped the question—and the world found out that Prince Charles was engaged to the soon-to-be Princess Diana of Wales. Once again, the newspapers and magazines started talking about how Diana and Charles were in love, and the country resurged in a fascination with "Shy Di."

Even Diana, who had been experiencing doubts about her relationship with Charles, once again found herself infatuated with the prince. Everyone in Diana's family supported her marriage—well, everyone except Frances, Diana's true mother. Frances and Diana took a trip to Australia, where they discussed Diana's future with Charles.

Frances suspected that, perhaps, things weren't quite right between Diana and Charles. She addressed a serious flaw in the courtship between the prince and soon-to-be princess: did Diana truly love Charles, or was she only fascinated with the idea of marrying a prince? Diana responded that she loved both of those ideas, and Frances's attempt to help Diana had failed entirely.

The media went crazy over the engagement between Diana and Charles. Diana had always loved being in front of the cameras, so she thought that she needed to look extra-beautiful— especially because more people would be paying attention to her. Newspapers and magazines and news stations around the worlds desperately wanted to cover every moment leading up to the big wedding.

Lady Diana moved into Buckingham Palace, the home of the royal family in Britain. Although it was only a temporary home, Diana loved it there. Of course, she *would* love it, since she had been dreaming of living in a place like the palace since she was a young child. She loved how big the palace was, and she loved the people that worked there.

Diana found the company of the royal family to be dry and boring. Instead, she loved talking to the maids and servants. Sometimes, she would sit on her bed for hours, talking with them about their lives. This made Diana much happier than talking with the royal family.

At first, Diana had been absolutely fascinated with Queen Elizabeth II. After all, she was the one who ruled an entire nation, whose family had gone back hundreds of years throughout England. But, as Diana soon figured out, the Queen was rarely seen. The Queen with several dozen people per day, and all of them treated her tremendously formally and professionally. After a while, the strict routines of palace life could get quite tiring. Because of this, the Queen often ate dinner alone in her bedroom, the television on, and her dinner tray resting on her lap.

Diana had always been searching for a female role model, and still she hoped to find on in the Queen—but Diana found no hope here since she barely ever saw Charles's mother.

In every wedding, the bride's wedding dress is often a center of attention. Everyone expected Diana to hire well-known designers to craft her wedding dress—but instead, she hired two unpopular designers. Everyone around her was quite surprised, but this was consistent with Diana's rebellious and unorthodox way of living.

The wedding between Diana and Charles was held in St. Paul's Cathedral, even though most of the royal weddings had occurred on Westminster Abbey. The couple chose St. Paul's Cathedral because it fit more people, so they could have a bigger wedding ceremony. In addition to that, the aisle at St. Paul's is longer, so it would take Diana longer to reach the altar—this way more people could take more pictures of her.

In the days leading up to the wedding, Diana was emotionally strained. She even had a few breakdowns. This was a sharp contrast to the way the world usually saw Diana—a very young, composed, calm and smiling girl. Crowds went wild over her, so it was unusual to see her cry.

But the wedding might not have been the only thing on her mind. Diana was jealous of another woman in Charles's life: Camilla Parker Bowles. Charles and Camilla spent a lot of time together, and Charles often bought her gifts. The two had been excellent friends since their younger years. Diana was always afraid that Charles secretly loved her.

In fact, the jealousy got so bad that Diana almost cancelled the wedding. After all the gifts that Charles was giving Camilla and all the attention he was showing her, Diana felt like she was left in the dust. She wanted to call the whole wedding off in a fury of jealous rage. But, unfortunately, all of the preparations had already been made; the wedding would go on, no matter what Diana wanted.

The date of the wedding was July 29th, 1981. On the morning of the wedding, Diana awoke to crowds of thousands of people waiting outside Buckingham Palace. They cheered and screamed when they saw her on her balcony. They all couldn't wait for the royal wedding to begin!

Diana contently got dressed. Her hair was done, and her make-up put on. Once she was fully prepared, a glass coach pulled up to Buckingham Palace, prepared to take her to St. Paul's Cathedral. Horses pulled her and her father, Johnnie, to the cathedral, where her soon-to-be husband and the royal family awaited her.

Johnnie walked Diana down the aisle, but Diana had more than the wedding on her mind. Recently, Johnnie had been quite ill after suffering from a stroke. As they stepped down the aisle of St. Paul's Cathedral, Diana had to support her father. But despite this, it was one of the proudest days of Johnnie's life.

The *trail* of a wedding dress is the part that brushes against the ground in the back. Oftentimes, the trail is long for a glamorous effect. Diana's, however, was extra big. It dragged twenty-five feet behind her! It was certainly a sight to see for everyone in the cathedral.

The wedding was glamorous and cost a lot of money. Specifically for the occasion, the royal couple had plates, mugs, and towels all made with their faces on them. This shows the wealth and grandeur of the royal family of Great Britain.

The wedding was not only a spectacular event within St. Paul's Cathedral. The momentous occasion was televised and broadcasted around the world. More than 750 million people—that's three-quarters of a *billion*!—watched the wedding of Diana and Charles. Diana would one day be the Queen of England, so this was a wedding that would change the course of the world.

Once the wedding ceremony was done, Diana's fantasy dream had come true. She was *finally* a princess—the princess of Wales, to be exact. Wales is a small country in the west of the island of England. Wales is part of the United Kingdom and Great Britain, and Charles rules as the Prince of Wales. Now, Diana was his princess, and one day she would rise to the Queen of a nation.

Following the ceremony, Diana and Charles briefly returned to Buckingham Palace. There, they stood on the balcony before the thousands of people crowding outside. All of these people were desperate for the slightest glimpse of Diana and Charles—it was a craze that gripped the entire nation, and the whole world.

The crowds cheered for Diana and Charles to share a kiss before the world. After all, the people and the media rarely saw any sign of affection within the royal family. A kiss would make the crowd go wild. Diana and Charles smiled at each other and kissed, and sure enough, the crowds exploded with joy and camera flashes.

Diana was tremendously excited for the honeymoon that followed the wedding. The first three days of the honeymoon were spent at a house called Broadland. Broadland had been in Charles's family for years, so it was meant to be a nice and quiet getaway for the busy couple.

After the time they spent on Broadland, Diana and Charles hopped on the *Brittania*, one of the royal family's yachts. The ship sailed around the Mediterranean Sea. The Mediterranean Sea coasts many countries, including Italy, Greece, Egypt, Spain, Libya, and Turkey. Diana was looking for private time with her husband, since they rarely saw each other without the pressuring cameras of the press or the watchful eyes of the royal family.

However, once again, Diana was disappointed. On the honeymoon, Charles was much more interested fishing than spending time with her. In addition to that, he had brought along a series of books on the subject of philosophy. He had asked her to read all of them, so that they could have dinner conversation on the books. But this was not Diana's idea of a vacation. After all, as a child, she did not do well in academic subjects. Her sisters had always been smarter, and the schools she attended focused more on social skills than schoolwork.

Reading philosophy for Charles was the *last* thing that Diana wanted to do. Charles, on the other hand, was a scholar. He found philosophy very interesting, and he loved to study and read. He and Diana could not have been more different on this matter.

To cope with the little affection that Charles was showing her, Diana did what she did best: she talked with people. She had never been a fan of the company of the royal family, but she instead liked the maids and servants. She spoke extensively with the yacht's staff, sometimes having conversations over delicious bowls of ice cream. She found them much more inviting and welcoming than Prince Charles.

Despite the fact that things never seemed to go the way that Diana had expected, she still made it through. No matter how Charles treated her, and no matter what she felt about him, she was still living her dream of being a princess. The Princess of Wales needed to be strong, and Diana would absolutely transform as she took on new roles and a whole new life as a princess.

Chapter 4: Royal Duties

Even as the royal wedding ended and Diana returned from her disappointing honeymoon, the media was still crazy about her. She had thought that people would calm down and leave her alone after the excitement of the wedding had passed—but people were just as interested in her as ever.

Prince Charles admitted that he was jealous of Diana's insane popularity. The photographers always mobbed her, leaving him alone. No photographers wanted pictures of Prince Charles, because those did not sell in the newspapers and magazines. Princess Diana, still called "Shy Di" was all the rage.

Now that she was a princess, Diana was entitled to all of the royal duties that came with the position. Most of the time, the royal family made public appearances and attended special meetings around the world. They are the face of the United Kingdom, and they must act as such. The British *Parliament*, kind of like America's *Congress*, makes laws, while the royal family rules the nation and meets with other world leaders.

Princess Diana mainly lived in the gorgeous Kensington Palace, which is situated in London. Whenever she and Charles wanted to escape for a small vacation, they would go to Highgrove, a house in Gloucestershire. Gloucestershire is a part of England. Highgrove was a favorite destination of Charles while Diana liked living in the city more.

Kensington Palace originated in 1689, when it was purchased by King William III. The palace has been the home of many famous members of the royal family. This includes Queen Victoria, who ruled during the 1800s.

Many of Diana's royal duties included charity work and, as she would soon realize, taking care of her soon-to-be born children.

Chapter 5: Children

As the future Queen of England, Diana had many important duties and meetings to attend. But a terribly important thing for her to realize was that her first child would one day become the King of England.

Charles is the son of Queen Elizabeth, which means that he will become the king after Elizabeth dies. Once Charles dies, his first-born son will take his place as the king. The world was watching Diana and Charles closely; their children would decide the fate of England.

Diana became pregnant in 1981, in the same year that she had been married. Her pregnancy was plagued with morning sickness, which is something that expecting mothers often feel. Oftentimes, morning sickness can bring about nausea and headaches. But Diana was strong, and this never stopped her from making her frequent public appearances. Diana was made for the camera, and nothing would ever hold her down.

As if the media could not harass Diana even more, the craze raged even more explosively after the news of her pregnancy reached the public. Despite the pressing cameras and the morning sickness, Diana still had the strength to make all of her commitments happen.

But *still*, the press wanted more.

Eventually, it got so bad that reporters and photographers were cornering and trapping her inside stores. The stress was unbelievable; when Diana knew that she would gain fame when she married Charles, this level of harassment was draining her emotionally and led to several breakdowns. After Diana was trapped in a candy store, the Queen was furious.

Queen Elizabeth had had quite enough. She was upset with the cameras, with the publicity, and the non-stop, constant news on the royal family. She invited all of the reporters in England to a special meeting. In this special meeting, the Queen asked the media to leave Diana alone. After all, she was pregnant, and the amount of attention she was getting was harassment. She wanted Diana to be left alone, so she can live her life normally.

But none of the journalists and reporters listened. Pictures of Diana sold for thousands of dollars each and every day, because of how popular she was.

Despite the franticness of the media, Diana continued dealing with her pregnancy. She began to plan the birth of her first son, but she had one small issue. Typically, babies of the royal family were born at home—without the use of hospital equipment and a host of doctors ready to help. It was simply tradition. But Diana was not such a fan of this rule.

Instead, she went to St. Mary's Hospital when she felt the baby coming. On June 21st, the first day of summer, of the year 1982, Diana's first son was born. From the moment he came into the world, Prince William's destiny was set. He was the first son of Diana and Charles, and he will one day rule the United Kingdom.

William was christened with the full name of William Arthur Philip Louis. Now, while the relationship between Diana and Charles may not have exactly been perfect, the two of them did make terrific parents. Each of them had come from homes with parents who were not attentive, loving, or affectionate. Because of this, Diana and Charles vowed to be the very best parents. They wanted to show William all of their love. In addition to that, they did not want him to have a strictly royal life. They wanted him to know what it was like to have a normal walk in the park, to have parents that showered him with kisses and love.

Of course, Diana and Charles needed to hire a nanny to take care of young William, but Diana made one thing real clear: *she* wanted to be the one to take care of William. She did not William to spend more time with a nanny than with her.

At the birth of the young prince, everyone in the world cheered, cried, and celebrated. However, a few months afterward, Diana felt hopelessly depressed. When at one point, everyone had wanted to know everything about her, now Prince William was the center of everyone's attention. The country's obsession was now the newborn child, and Diana felt jealous and lonely.

When William was only nine months old, Diana and Charles were scheduled to venture on a tour of Australia and New Zealand, making several public appearances along the way. William, since he was an infant, was not allowed to go on the trip, and this upset Diana and Charles. After all, they remembered when their parents were gone for long stretches of time. It took a toll on their childhood, and they blamed their parents' absences for creating emotional problems. For this reason, Diana and Charles actually wanted to take William with them.

Diana made a special request to Queen Elizabeth, asking her if William could attend the trip, as well. The Queen recognized Diana's reasons and accepted. Prince William was the first infant to ever go on a tour with members of the royal family! The tour was also a massive success. People loved seeing them.

Just a few years later, Diana became pregnant with her second child. This pregnancy was not as painful as the first. She still experienced morning sickness, but it was nothing that she couldn't handle. Diana was also happy that Charles had agreed to spend more time with her, and with the children. He wanted to put his family before his work, which had always been a problem in the past.

Diana's second child was born on September 15th, 1984. While the world immediately rejoiced, Prince Charles was rather disappointed. He had always wanted to be the father of a baby girl, but the child was a boy. And if that wasn't enough, the boy had ginger hair, which had been commonly seen in Diana's family. Charles was not pleased, which made Diana extremely upset.

The child was christened Harry Charles Albert David. Prince William and Prince Harry, although neither of them had reached the age of five, both stood as members of the royal family. Children around the world dream of being princes, and these two children have been in the royal family since the day they were born.

Despite the disappointment that Charles first showed when he saw his son William, the two of them grew to have a close relationship. Charles was only upset and reacted emotionally in the heat of the moment. He loves his son very much!

Now, it is a rule in England that the *first-born* son will inherit the throne. If the Queen dies, then her son Charles will take over. And if Charles dies, then his first-son Prince William takes the throne. So what happens to Prince Harry? Well, if William ever dies or is unable to rule the kingdom, then Harry will take his place. It may seem like there would be a heated rivalry between the two brothers, but the two of them are actually great friends and are involved in a lot of charity.

Chapter 6: Charity

Charity has been hugely popular among the royal family recently. *Charity* is helping those in need, and those who are less fortunate than you. Since the royal family is extremely wealthy and live in fancy palaces, there is plenty of room for them to be charitable.

Princess Diana set the bar very high when going out into other countries and performing charitable acts. Her people skills made her a shining angel wherever she walked. She spent a lot of time with people who were disabled, both physically and mentally. She understood she was much more fortunate than other people, so she wanted to help out as much as possible.

Diana worked with patients who were afflicted with AIDS. *AIDS* is an acronym for Acquired Immune Deficiency. The immune system is what keeps our bodies safe from viruses and infections, and AIDS makes the immune system weak. This means that people are more likely to become ill. AIDS became known during the 1980s, so this syndrome was extremely relevant during Diana's time. It still affects many people today, but scientists are searching for a cure. In the 1980s, many people were frightened.

Why were people frightened? Well, some people thought that AIDS could spread simply by being near a person, or by touching them. Now, we know that this is not true. But in the 1980s, fear was rampant. Princess Diana helped open a section of a British hospital that was specifically devoted for the treatment of patients with AIDS.

The hospital asked Diana if she would touch and shake hands with the patients there. The doctors thought that if the world saw Diana interacting with patients, then people would not be so afraid. Diana immediately agreed. With no gloves and no mask over her mouth, she walked into the ward and shook hands with the patients.

Pictures of the princess with the patients were on the front page of newspapers and magazines around the world. For everyone, this was something revolutionary. Just by shaking the hands of patients, Diana changed the way that people viewed the infection. No longer were most people afraid to go near people with AIDS. Diana altered the way people thought.

As a kid, Diana had always preferred talking and spending time with staff members than the rich royal family. Likewise, she had no problem spending hours upon hours just talking with the patients, discussing their lives. People loved seeing that a member of the royal family—especially the future Queen of England—could be so caring and affectionate. Her travels across the world were extremely influential. Everywhere, people saw her doing good deeds. They were inspired to do the same.

Towards the end of the 1980s, Diana hopped on a plane and traveled to New York in the United States of America. She wanted to visit the state's many homeless people, which had been a growing issue.

Princess Diana visited a homeless shelter on Henry Street in New York. This shelter had seen many celebrities and politicians come through, all of them trying to make it seem like they visited the homeless. However, oftentimes, the celebrities and politicians would arrive, take pictures with the owners of the shelter, and leave. Diana was determined to make a stronger impression, whether the cameras were taking pictures or not. This was something truly special about Diana: she would not act good just for the cameras and the reporters. She genuinely cared about the people she visited.

At the shelter, she was dying to meet the children and the families. It must have been odd, to see all of the homeless people of New York, when she lived in such a rich and fancy palace in one of the world's greatest cities.

Diana affected the world with her charity. Everyone continued to be obsessed over the princess—so obsessed, in fact, that even Prince Charles's charity was utterly forgotten. Of course, Prince Charles was generous and philanthropic. But no one paid attention to this. Instead, the media dubbed him as a snobbish, rich member of the royal of the family. This was a stark contrast to "Shy Di," who was adored by people everywhere.

The differences between Diana and Charles, as well as how newspapers and magazines portrayed them, would lead to a rift in their relationship. Their courtship and marriage had never been perfect, but now it was truly falling apart. In the months to come, Diana's rage would become fiercer than ever as her children became involved and affected in Charles's selfishness. She wanted a perfect life for William and Harry, so she hated to see Charles going down the emotionless path that his own parents had gone down.

While it is easy to see Charles as the bad guy, it is important to understand that he and Diana were two completely different people, with two decidedly different lifestyles. Their separation could have easily been foretold since the day they met. Soon enough, their relationship would collapse, and divorce would lie in their future.

Chapter 7: Divorce and Life After Divorce

Through all of the charities and the royal duties, Diana's relationship problems persisted. Most of these issues arose because of Charles's busy schedule, and his lack of affection towards her and their children.

Charles and Diana sent William and Harry to boarding schools. The two children would stay at these boarding schools throughout the entire week, and only saw their parents on weekends. During the weekends, Diana, William, and Henry would drive up to Highgrove, where Charles was staying. But at Highgrove, Charles much preferred to spend time alone. It was Diana that spent the most time with her kids, and because of this, she built a strong relationship with the two young princes.

But the world did not need Diana's opinion to know that Prince Charles was acting like a poor father. It seemed that time and time again, he would always choose work over his children. He would always choose his own interests over Diana's. This made Diana angry—and the media saw all of the trouble that came from this.

People ridiculed Prince Charles for his quirkiness and his constantly negative attitude. While Diana and her children always wore smiles on their faces, it was much harder to find Charles happy. Because of this, people liked Diana much more. They loved picking up a magazine and seeing "Shy Di's" gorgeous and smiling face.

One day, an event rocked the Royal Family that would destroy Prince Charles's reputation. On a golfing trip, the young Prince William was accidentally struck in the head with a golf club. His skull was fractured, and he needed to be rushed to the hospital. At the hospital, only Diana stayed with William. Charles, instead, left and attended an opera performance. People were *furious* with Charles—while his son sat in the hospital, awaiting surgery, he was at the opera.

Prince Charles attempted to justify his actions. He said that the injury was minor, and that he knew William would be fine. But even if the injury was minor, people were outraged that a father would leave his son in the hospital. Diana, secretly, was happy to see Charles leave. There was no way she wanted Charles in the hospital, making negative comments and bringing down all hope.

Their marriage was collapsing. Perhaps both of them knew this, but they did not want to admit it.

Diana was struck emotionally, and suddenly, when she learned of her father's death. She was on a trip in Australia with Prince Charles when the news came to her, and she was completely devastated. She knew that she must fly back to England immediately. Charles, wishing to be a good husband, told her that he would come with her. Diana, however, did want Charles to come. It was royal policy that Charles must come with her, which made Diana furious. Together, Princess Diana and Prince Charles took a plane back to England.

Diana's brother, also named Charles, was now the owner of Althorp, their family house. Charles Spencer was now called the *Earl Spencer*, which had been the title held by Johnnie, their newly-deceased father.

The emotional stress and the arguments between Charles and Diana soon became too much for them to handle. On November 25th, 1992, Charles told Diana that he did not want to be with her anymore. While the two of them did not wish to be *divorced*, they did want to be separated. A divorce would cause too much trouble in the royal family. Charles and Diana were allowed to keep their marriage, but not be obliged to love each other.

Diana was afraid that William and Harry would find out about the divorce from the newspapers and magazines, since news traveled so quickly. She quickly went to William and Harry, and she personally and calmly told them that she and their father were separating.

Diana recalled that the toughest part of the separation was being away from her two children. Princess Diana and Prince Charles now had to divide their time between William and Harry, which put a strain on both Diana and the children. Since William and Harry were at boarding school during the week, they were only allowed to see their parents on weekends. On one weekend, they would see Charles, then they would go back to school. The next weekend, they would stay with Diana. This cycle would repeat endlessly. Diana did not like this at all. Her love for her children was undying, and she missed them terribly.

But, still, Diana remained as strong as ever. She never let any emotional troubles bring her down. She powered through all of the royal duties. Even though she and Prince Charles were separated, they were still technically married. Diana was still a princess, and she still needed to commit to her royal duties.

And her presence in the public came the media. Reporters and photographers still followed Diana everywhere she went. Her public appearances continued as usual, and so did all of her charitable acts. Diana even joined forces with the International Red Cross, a charity organization. The International Red Cross helps victims of war, and this was a charity that Diana really wanted to assist. Her work never went unphotographed, and the effect that she had on other parts of the world are incredible.

In addition to her charity work, Princess Diana still met with many world leaders. Her public appearances made people go crazy, even after all these years. Although she was not *with* Prince Charles, the people and the media loved her no matter what. She was an idol and a model for all to see. Photographs of Diana sold for thousands of dollars, since they were printed on newspapers and magazines across the world. A magazine with good pictures of Diana would sell like crazy.

Because of this, many people even tried to photograph her in private. One time, she was exercising at the gym, and someone took a picture of her—a picture that she thought was extremely unattractive. This was an invasion of privacy that disturbed both Diana and the rest of the royal family. Diana always wondered what she could do to get her normal life back. She loved the cameras and the reporters, but sometimes it became too much for her to handle.

Diana recognized that there was no way to escape the media, even after her separation with Charles. To the disappointment of millions of people across the world, Diana announced that she no longer wished to make public appearances. She wanted to live in private for a while, without the flashing cameras, the screaming journalists, and the cheering crowds. Everything was becoming too overwhelming, and she badly needed a break. This also meant that she needed to reduce the charity work she did.

Part of Diana's rise to popularity had been based on her charity. People loved seeing a member of the royal family dressed in work clothes, serving food to victims of war, or playing chess with sick patients. It was what made her so attractive. She was part of the royal family, but she showed that even the richest people could help the least fortunate. This must have been a tough decision for Diana, since she liked her charity work so much. This also must have been tough for the world to see, since they realized there was no way to stop the paparazzi and the reporters. The more that people read magazines about Diana, the more that reporters would harass her for pictures. And the more that reporters harassed her for pictures, the more she wanted to live a private life. It was a complicated situation.

After years of emotional stress and pressure, Diana decided that she finally wanted an official divorce from Prince Charles. The divorce was finalized on August 28th, 1996. Now, Diana lost her title of "Her Royal Highness." This meant that she was no longer a part of the royal family, but Queen Elizabeth said that Diana could still be a princess.

Despite that Diana was still called Princess Diana, people around the world were outraged. They wanted Diana to still be a part of the royal family, even if she was divorced from Prince Charles. People knew that Diana was doing a lot of good in the world, and she gave the royal family a good image. People said that Queen Elizabeth did not like the trouble that Diana's popularity caused, so she did want Diana to be a part of the royal family anymore. The media took Diana's side. It seems like the only people against Diana were Prince Charles and Queen Elizabeth.

Still, Diana was strong. She knew that she would need to power through the divorce. She wondered if the divorce would mean that her life was calmer. Every day, she wondered whether the reporters and photographers would ever leave her alone. Even if they didn't, the divorce from Prince Charles brought a lot of happiness to her life. She was finally free of the man had caused her so much pain and stress.

Diana loved working for charity, so she decided to start again. With the International Red Cross, she helped victims of landmines. *Landmines* are harmful bombs that are placed in the ground. In other countries, many people are hurt by these every day, and Diana wanted to help.

She spent time in the country of Angola, which is in southern Africa. While she was there, she helped film a documentary with a news station. The news station is called BBC, or the British Broadcasting Corporation. It is one of Britain's most popular television networks. While there, Diana made sure to not show that she was rich. She ate the same food as everyone else, she wore the same clothes as everyone else, and people loved the way she acted. Diana never failed to impress the world.

Diana's stay in Angola brought attention to the problems of landmines. People saw how dangerous they were, and they saw that even the royal Princess Diana was willing to help out.

Slowly, Diana's life began to come together again—but not for long. At least for a while, she felt truly happy doing her charity work. Even within the royal family, her shattered relationship with Charles was improving. Even though they were divorced, the Prince and Princess became great friends once again. After all, they had two sons together. It would be silly for them not to be friends.

During all of this time, Diana wanted to have other boyfriends. She wanted other romantic options. One boyfriend, Hasnat Khan, was not too nice to her, so they quickly broke up. The media followed Diana's relationships by the moment. Almost every moment of her life was followed, reported, quoted, photographed, or televised.

Diana really wanted an escape from the stress of her relationship with Hasnat Khan. She was supremely happy when she was invited on a vacation by Mohamed Al Fayed. He was an Egyptian businessman who owned a line of department stores in Britain, and he had a son named Dodi. His hope was that Diana and Dodi would meet, and they would become interested in each other.

Diana took a plane to St. Tropez, a part of France. She came with William and Harry, and they all stayed on the *Jonikal*, which was the yacht of Al Fayed. Of course, Diana and Dodi hit it off right away, just like Al Fayed wanted. Dodi was charming and attractive. He was forty-one years old, and he was not married, so Diana saw him as a perfect match.

Chapter 8: Death and Legacy

Diana had no idea what was soon to happen. Her life seemed to be going normally: her relationship with Dodi made her truly happy, and the media was just as crazy as ever. A couple months after Dodi and Diana had met, the two of them decided to venture on another vacation on Dodi's father's yacht. After the vacation, the two of them decided to spend some time in Paris, the capital of France.

Diana planned for their Paris trip to be short and sweet. She was anxious to return to London to see William and Harry. After all, they would be returning to school soon, and she wanted to spend as much time with her two sons as possible.

Even in the gorgeous and bright city of Paris, however, Diana could not escape the paparazzi. She and Dodi arrived in the city on August 31st, 1997 to swarms of reporters and photographers—everyone wanted a picture of the princess and her boyfriend. To escape the crazy masses, Diana and Dodi checked into the Ritz, a fancy and luxurious hotel in Paris. While Diana was not one for luxury, Dodi liked spending a lot of money.

She and Dodi rented a room for the night. She enjoyed the peace and quiet of the room, after being chased by the paparazzi on the way to the hotel. Dodi said he would be right back, and he left the room. He wanted to go across the street to buy Diana some jewelry. Some people think that Dodi wanted to buy Diana an engagement ring. The two of them liked each other so much, rumors were flying about a potential engagement and marriage. Dodi only spent a few minutes in the store, so no one is quite sure exactly what he meant to do.

When Dodi returned to the hotel room, he and Diana decided they would go to his apartment, but they did not stay there long. A couple hours after riding through crowds of photogrraphers and paparazzi and staying at the apartment, Diana and Dodi left. It was about 9:30 PM, and they were both hungry for dinner.

Their dinner plans were ruined, however. They tried to take a taxi to a fancy restaurant, but the paparazzi is swarming the vehicle from all sides and the back. There would have been no way for Dodi and Diana to even exit the vehicle. The stress levels rose incredibly; all Diana wanted was a normal night. They decided that they will go back to the Ritz, since the hotel was safe and quiet from the flashing cameras and screams of the paparazzi.

But even the dinner at the Ritz was a failure. Diana and Dodi kept getting stares from everyone around them, and they both quickly lost their appetite. They asked the staff members to take their meal up to their room—but the two of them never went back to their room.

Diana and Dodi no longer wanted to stay in the hotel. No one was sure exactly why they wanted to leave—perhaps they wanted to leave Paris altogether. The paparazzi was too much for either of them to handle. So, they left the hotel and pushed into the screaming crowds surrounding the hotel.

Henri Paul was with Diana and Dodi that night. Henri Paul was their driver, and some people even blame him for Diana and Dodi's deaths. Unfortunately, Henri Paul had been drinking alcohol that night, and it is illegal to drink alcohol and then drive. Drinking and driving can make using a car extremely dangerous; it put everyone's life in danger. Also with them was Trevor Rees-Jones, who was Dodi's personal bodyguard.

By the time Henri Paul pulled the car up to the front of the Ritz, it was past midnight. It was now August 31st, 1997. Paul drove away, and the paparazzi quickly followed. They drove in cars after Diana, they rode bicycles, and they ran. They were all desperate for pictures of her—they simply could not get enough. The paparazzi were greedy, and they did not respect Diana's privacy.

Dodi told Henri Paul to escape the paparazzi at all costs. Henri Paul started to go seventy miles over the speed limit. He drove through red lights, didn't stop at stop signs, and he also wasn't wearing a seatbelt. In fact, no one in car was wearing a seatbelt except the bodyguard. This was a mistake that would lead to tragic circumstances. Henri Paul drove like a madman, desperate to be free of the cars that were chasing him.

Paul was driving so quickly that he hit a bump in the road, and the entire car almost flew into the air. He was driving so fast that he could not stop before he hit another car. Paul's car spun around and slammed into a wall. The car was smashed.

Both Dodi and Henri Paul died immediately. Trevor-Rees, the bodyguard, and Princess Diana were still alive, though. Diana had been knocked out. The paparazzi quickly caught up to the car. Instead of rushing to see if everyone was okay, the paparazzi did not help Diana. Instead, they took as many pictures of the wreckage as possible.

An ambulance came quickly, though. Within six minutes, paramedics had arrived and were taking Diana back to the hospital. She was bleeding internally, which is extremely dangerous. A couple hours later, Princess Diana of Wales was pronounced dead.

The royal family was told immediately. At first, Prince Charles just heard that Diana had been injured. He was surprised. But when news came that Diana had died, Charles began to cry like he never had before.

The world cried with Prince Charles that fateful morning. Outside of Kensington Palace, *thousands* of flowers were laid on the ground in Diana's honor. More than just flowers were placed there, though: small stuffed animals, letters, pictures, candles, and anything that could be used to express emotion and pay tribute to one of the world's greatest women.

Many people were upset at Queen Elizabeth after Diana's death, since she did not show that she was said. Firstly, she ordered Prince Charles that he was not allowed to bring Diana's body home from Paris. Secondly, the flag outside Buckingham Palace was not lowered to half-mast. When a bad event happens, and a country mourns the loss of someone, flags are lowered halfway down the pole. This signifies that a tragedy has happened. People were terribly upset that the flag stayed at the top of the pole.

Diana's funeral happened a few days later, on September 6th, 1997. Her coffin was decorated with beautiful flowers. It was escorted in a carriage through the streets of London. People lined the streets by the thousands. They were all sad for Diana. Diana's death was not just a loss for England; it was a loss for the entire world.

The funeral ceremony was shown on television, so that people around the Earth could mourn for the loss of Princess Diana. The funeral ceremony was watched by more than 2.5 billion people; only 750 million people watched the marriage between Charles and Diana. After the ceremony, which took place at Westminster Abbey, Diana's body was taken back to Althorp, her childhood home. Near Althorp, there was a small lake with an island in the middle. Diana was buried on this island. It was quiet, private, and peaceful—just like Diana would have wanted.

Even now, her legacy lives on. Her charity work and her love for everyone has not died. Still, people are inspired by the wonderful work that she did while she was alive. Her two sons, William and Harry, are still alive, and they are enjoying their lives as princes. Prince William and Prince Harry know how much their mother was involved in charity, and they both have taken steps to do their own charity work. William and Harry have helped victims of AIDS, something their mother helped with, as well.

Tributes to Diana appeared all over England. In London, you can visit the Princess Diana Memorial Walk. It is a trail that lasts for seven miles and visits many places that were significant in Diana's life. In Hyde Park in London, tourists and fans of Diana can look the gorgeous Princess Diana Memorial Fountain. Diana's memory is now permanently imprinted on the streets of London. She will never be forgotten by the world.

Bibliography

Brown, Tina. *The Diana Chronicles*. New York: Doubleday, 2007. Print.

Mattern, Joanne. *Princess Diana*. New York: DK Pub., 2006. Print.

29750506R00053